The Best-Ever Book of
DINOSAURS

Michael Benton

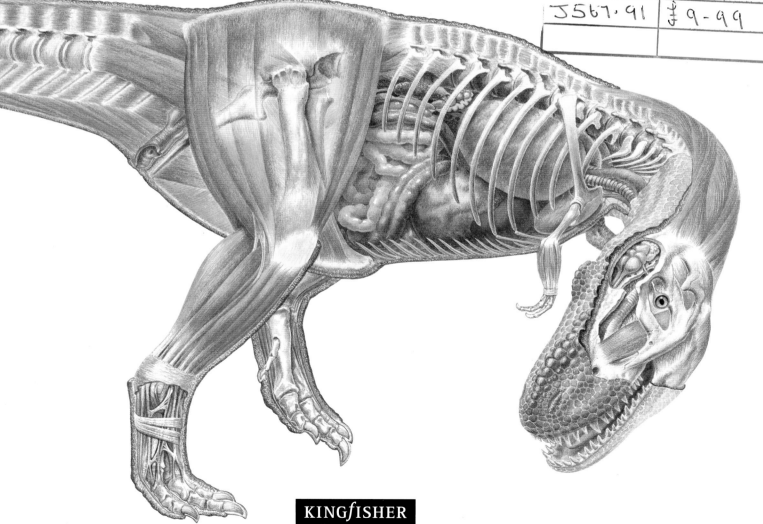

KINGFISHER

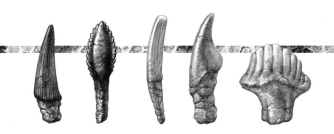

KINGFISHER
Kingfisher Publications Plc
New Penderel House, 283–288 High Holborn,
London WC1V 7HZ

First published by Kingfisher Publications Plc 1998

10 9 8 7 6 5 4

4(TR)0200/SIN/PW/128MA

Copyright © Kingfisher Publications Plc 1998

A CIP catalogue record for this book is
available from the British Library.

ISBN 0 7534 0219 X

Managing editor: Molly Perham
Series editor: Camilla Hallinan
Design: Malcolm Smythe, Ben White, Terry Woodley
Cover design: Terry Woodley
Picture research: Veneta Bullen
Printed in Hong Kong / China

ABOUT THE AUTHOR

Professor Michael Benton works at the University of
Bristol, and travels far and wide – recently he has taken
expeditions to Romania (for fragments of pterosaurs and
dinosaurs in ancient caves) and Russia (for pre-dinosaur
remains in the South Urals). He has also written over 30
books on dinosaurs, and was a consultant on the
Learning Channel's *Paleoworld* series in the US.

◄ A team of fossil
hunters takes a break
at the Flaming Cliffs in
Mongolia, China, where
dinosaurs once nested.

As you turn the pages,
look out for a baby
Maiasaura from
Montana, USA. See it
hatch from its egg, get
its first meal, leave the
nest, meet a hungry
T rex, and run back to
the safety of the herd.

CONTENTS

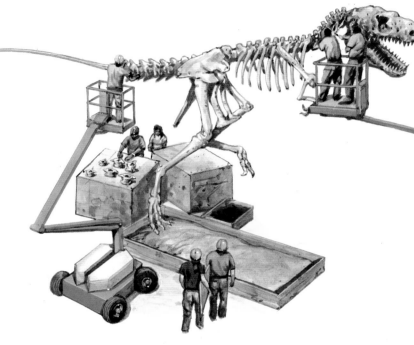

FINDING OUT

Digging up dinosaurs is hard, dirty work. Bone collectors toil for weeks to dig up a dinosaur skeleton. Then teams of palaeontologists, the experts who study fossils, spend months or even years putting the bones together. Their painstaking work makes it possible to reconstruct scenes like the one on the cover of this book – it shows the giant flesh-eater *Tyrannosaurus* racing across a mudflat to attack a *Struthiomimus* seventy million years ago.

▲ A fossil is the remains of an animal or plant that lived millions of years ago. When a dinosaur died, its skeleton became covered in sand or soil, or was washed away and broken up by a river. Here, in Montana, USA, a bone collector is chipping at the rock to reveal a large fossilized bone.

Prospecting

Dinosaur hunters prospect a site by walking over the ground looking for tell-tale clues. A skilled collector can spot a fragment of bone 100 metres away. When a bone is found, the collector must decide whether it is worth following up. Often the first report of a new site comes from an amateur collector who calls in the local museum to investigate.

▲ The dinosaur collectors set up basecamp, a group of trailers or tents where they sleep and keep supplies. On a small site, there will be a team of about ten people. They are usually volunteers — some are palaeontologists, others are students.

▼ Dinosaur collectors often work in remote places. They can find and record their exact location by using a Global Positioning System (GPS) on a portable computer. The GPS bounces signals to satellites that are in fixed positions out in space. Signals echoed back from at least three satellites fix the position of the GPS computer exactly.

It is important to know where a dinosaur is found, for two reasons. Collectors may need to return to the site later on, to look for more fossils. And they will study the history of the site when they return to their museums – where a fossil is found can reveal as much about the dinosaur's life and times as the fossil does.

◄ Dinosaur skeletons are buried in rock. The team must drill into the rock lying above the skeleton, called the overburden, and take it away. They use mechanical diggers and bulldozers, and even explosives when there is very thick rock.

▲ The collectors keep a detailed record of all the bones. They map their position using a grid made from string, and draw each bone on a scaled-down version of the grid on paper. This will help them to put the skeleton together later on, at the museum.

1. Uncovering

Once the overburden is removed, the collectors use fine needles and picks to scrape the rock and expose the bones. They brush away dust as they work. The bones are strengthened by filling all the hollow spaces with glue.

2. Clearing

When a bone is completely cleared and exposed on the rock surface, it is identified and mapped. Then the collectors work out where to look for more bones.

Digging up dinosaurs

Early bone hunters worked very fast, using explosives and heavy equipment to get the huge fossils out of the rock. Today, collectors use their equipment more carefully. Dinosaur bones may be big, but they can also be fragile. One false move, and they are shattered. When students go on their first dinosaur dig, they must be trained in all the field techniques. Modern technology and chemicals help make their task easier.

3. Digging channels

Channels are dug around the bone so that it stands on a pedestal. It is now ready to be wrapped.

4. Protecting

First the bone is covered with strips of wet paper, so that the next layer of plaster won't stick to and damage the bone.

5. Plastering
Strips of sackcloth, or burlap, are soaked in liquid plaster. Then they are laid over the protective layer of damp paper.

6. More plastering
Five or six layers of plaster strips are built up until the bone is well covered. This will make a hard cast to hold the bone together.

7. Hardening
Any gaps and hollows are filled with more plaster and the whole parcel is smoothed over. The plaster is left to dry and harden.

8. Turning
The pedestal is chipped away using picks and chisels. Then the bone is turned so that the other side can be plastered.

Using radar
Ground-penetrating radar (GPR) is a surveying system that detects differences in density. Bones can be detected in soil because of their greater density. But rock and bone have similar density, so radar works less well in rock.

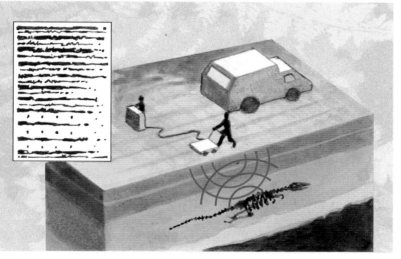

Is there any way of finding bones buried deep in the rock without digging? Some dinosaur bones in the American Midwest contain uranium. Because uranium is radioactive, a geiger counter can detect the bones. What the collector sees is glowing bones!

9. Moving
The collecting team takes the plaster parcels back to the basecamp. They pull them along on wooden runners, or lift them with mechanical equipment. At the end of the season, they load the bones onto trucks and drive back to the museum laboratory.

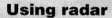

Bringing dinosaurs to life

In the museum laboratory, a team of technicians and scientists cleans up the bones, identifies them and tries to put together a skeleton. Some finds consist of fragments of a known dinosaur. Others may be from an entirely new species.

The next step is to try to reconstruct what the dinosaur looked like when it was alive. Bringing dinosaurs to life requires a mixture of science and art. Scientists study how modern animals walk and run. Designers use computers to simulate a roaring, running dinosaur.

2. Making casts

Putting fragile bones on display is very risky. The technicians cover each bone with soft plastic. When this has set, they peel it off to produce a mould shaped like the bone. Then the mould is filled with a light and strong material such as fibreglass or plastic, to make a copy, or cast, of the original bone.

3. Painting

Casts can be made to look like the original bone. The plastic solution is coloured a natural brown or grey before it is poured into the mould. When the mould is peeled off, the cast can be painted to make it look real. Often it is impossible to tell the cast from the real thing!

1. Extracting and strengthening

Technicians use small power saws to cut off the plaster casts. They then clean the bones by carefully picking, drilling and brushing off all the remaining rock. The cleaned bones are strengthened with a special glue, and broken pieces are repaired. A large set of bones, such as a skull, may be in many separate fragments.

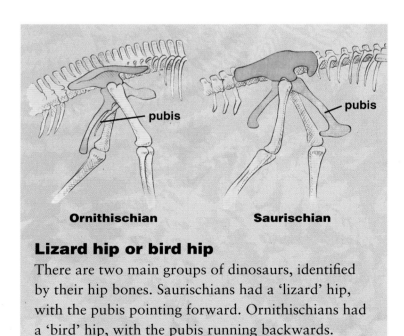

Ornithischian

Saurischian

Lizard hip or bird hip

There are two main groups of dinosaurs, identified by their hip bones. Saurischians had a 'lizard' hip, with the pubis pointing forward. Ornithischians had a 'bird' hip, with the pubis running backwards.

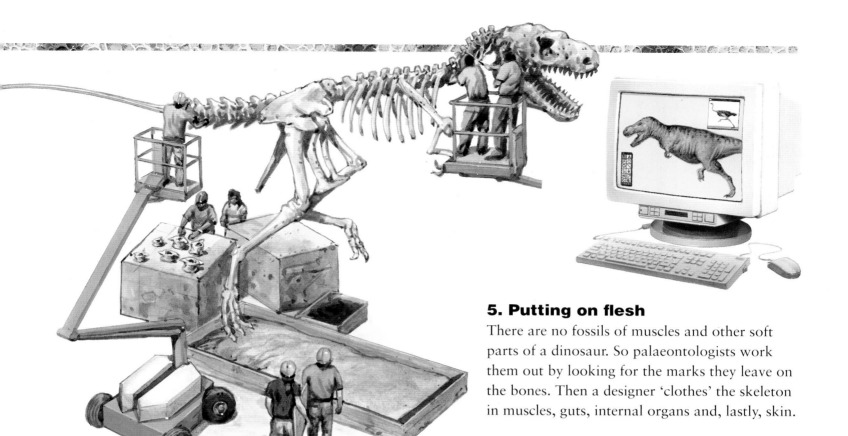

5. Putting on flesh

There are no fossils of muscles and other soft parts of a dinosaur. So palaeontologists work them out by looking for the marks they leave on the bones. Then a designer 'clothes' the skeleton in muscles, guts, internal organs and, lastly, skin.

▼ Life-size models are made from fibreglass or rubber. To choose a colour, designers look at modern animals and take a guess.

4. Constructing

For a new display, technicians mount some whole skeletons. They build a framework by welding thin strips of metal together, and then fix the bones to it. If plastic casts are used instead of bones, the framework can be hidden inside the casts. The skeleton of a *Tyrannosaurus* is so huge that it has to be assembled on the site of the exhibition – it takes days to fit all the bones together.

Dinosaurs are often the most popular part of a museum. A big exhibition, with skeletons, moving models and films, can take two or three years to prepare, and travel around the world. Exhibitions are a good way to tell the public about new discoveries. The money they raise helps to fund new expeditions.

6. Spreading the news

New ideas are published on the Internet and in books and scientific journals, so that people all over the world can share the information. The reconstructions of dinosaurs you see in this book are the result of new ideas and modern technology.

▼ Some flesh-eating *Ceratosaurus* stalk a herd of plant-eating *Apatosaurus*. Moving as a herd protects the young dinosaurs in the middle. But the *Ceratosaurus* hope to separate a young *Apatosaurus* – or an old and weak one – from the herd so that they can attack it and kill it.

▲ Two pterosaurs, *Rhamphorhynchus*, survey the scene below. On the left, some plate-backed *Stegosaurus* are drinking at the edge of the river. A long-necked *Diplodocus* is crossing to feed on plants on the same bank. On the right, a herd of *Barosaurus* heads for new grazing among the trees.

THE WORLD OF DINOSAURS

In the Late Jurassic period 150 million years ago, forests of lush vegetation flourished in the tropical climate of the American Midwest. Herds of large, plant-eating dinosaurs moved slowly along the banks of the rivers, stalked by fierce flesh-eaters. By studying the Morrison Formation, a thick unit of rock that is found over large areas of Utah and Colorado, palaeontologists have been able to reconstruct the world of these dinosaurs in amazing detail.

▼ Two flesh-eating *Allosaurus* have cornered a *Diplodocus*. They will try to snatch hunks of flesh and then follow the *Diplodocus* as it bleeds to death. But killing such a huge plant-eater is not easy. *Diplodocus* can whirl and stamp on *Allosaurus*, or lash out with its tail.

The bone hunters
From 1870 to the 1890s, Othniel Charles Marsh (centre back row, with his collectors) and Edward Drinker Cope (right) competed to find the best skeletons at the Morrison Formation.

Before the dinosaurs

Dinosaurs are relatively modern animals. Life existed on Earth for millions of years before dinosaurs came on the scene. The first living things were microscopic bacteria that lived in the sea 3,500 million years ago.

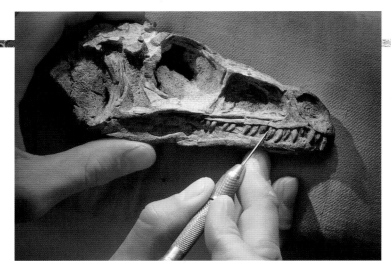

The first dinosaurs

The oldest dinosaurs, such as *Eoraptor* (above), were human-sized flesh-eaters. The rocks in which the *Eoraptor* fossils were found are 228 million years old. The skull has pointed, curved teeth for tearing flesh.

▼ By 520 million years ago larger sea creatures appeared. In the Burgess Shale of Canada there were weird animals with jointed legs, which were distant relatives of crabs. *Pikaia* was the first fish and the first vertebrate or animal with a backbone.

▼ Great changes took place 380 million years ago during the Devonian period. Life moved onto land.

Plants, insects and the first amphibians appeared – *Ichthyostega* was an ancestor of frogs and salamanders.

Pikaia

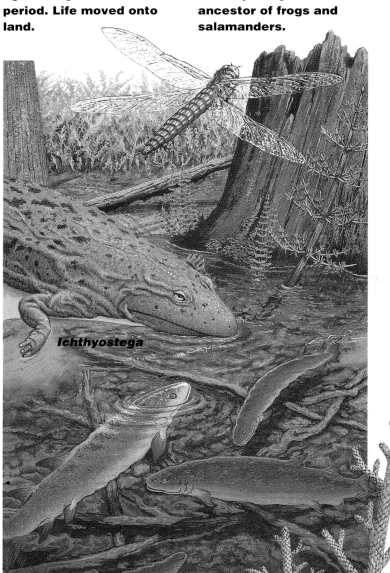

Ichthyostega

The Earth was formed as a molten ball of rock about 4,600 million years ago. It took at least 600 million years to cool down. The first living things appeared 3,500 million years ago, but they remained microscopic until about 600 million years ago. After that, life in the sea diversified to include corals, fishes, shellfish and the ancestors of crabs.

The next big step was the move onto land. The first back-boned animals on land, the amphibians, still laid their eggs in water. Then, 320 million years ago, came the reptiles – their eggs have a protective shell because they are laid on land. The first dinosaurs appeared when nineteen-twentieths of Earth's history had already passed!

▼ Reptiles were common during the Permian period, 260 million years ago. *Lycaenops* was a mammal-like reptile, an ancestor of modern mammals. This sabre-toothed predator could kill thick-skinned plant-eaters like *Scutosaurus*.

▼ A mass extinction wiped out many species at the end of the Permian period, 250 million years ago. By Late Triassic times 225 million years ago, the first dinosaurs, such as *Eoraptor*, and the first mammals, such as *Megazostrodon*, appeared.

Lycaenops

Scutosaurus

Eoraptor

Megazostrodon

Moving continents

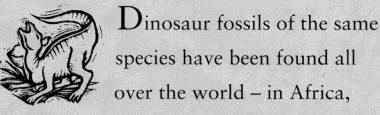

Dinosaur fossils of the same species have been found all over the world – in Africa, North America, Europe and Australia. This is a bit like finding a lion in Australia. But geologists have shown that the continents used to be joined together as a single great landmass called Pangaea ('All-Earth'). So the dinosaurs could roam right across the globe.

First life
3,500
mya

(mya = million
years ago)

ORDOVICIAN

SILURIAN

First
multi-
celled
life 1,200
mya

▶ Earth's geological timescale, or life story, has a long Precambrian era, when living things were simple and mostly very small. After that come three eras when fossils become much more common – the Palaeozoic ('ancient life'), Mesozoic ('middle life') and Cenozoic ('recent life').

DEVONIAN

CARBONIFEROUS

▼ The best-known dinosaur fossil sites are in North America and Europe, and in China and Mongolia in Asia. Recently, exciting new fossils have also been found in Australia, South Africa and Antarctica.

First
amphibians
380 mya

First
reptiles
320 mya

- CRETACEOUS

- JURASSIC

- TRIASSIC

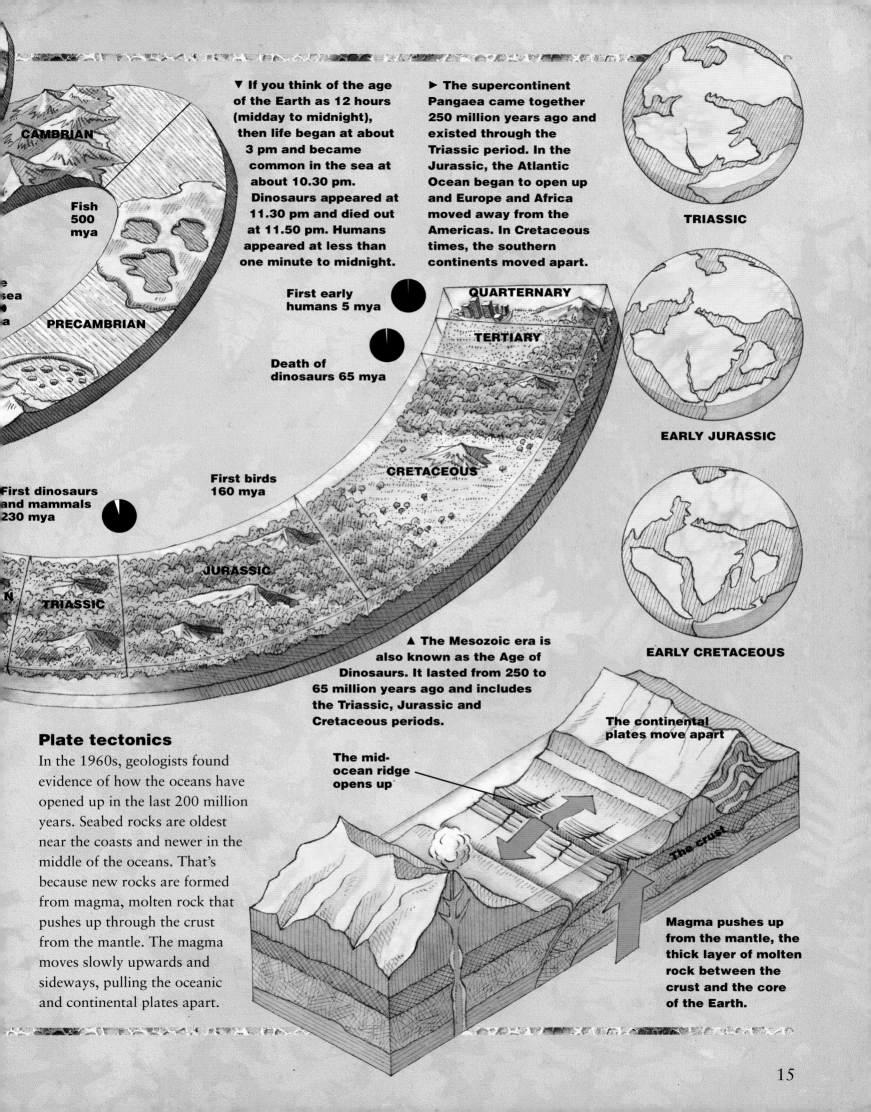

CAMBRIAN

Fish
500
mya

PRECAMBRIAN

▼ If you think of the age of the Earth as 12 hours (midday to midnight), then life began at about 3 pm and became common in the sea at about 10.30 pm. Dinosaurs appeared at 11.30 pm and died out at 11.50 pm. Humans appeared at less than one minute to midnight.

► The supercontinent Pangaea came together 250 million years ago and existed through the Triassic period. In the Jurassic, the Atlantic Ocean began to open up and Europe and Africa moved away from the Americas. In Cretaceous times, the southern continents moved apart.

TRIASSIC

First early humans 5 mya

QUARTERNARY

TERTIARY

Death of dinosaurs 65 mya

CRETACEOUS

EARLY JURASSIC

First birds 160 mya

First dinosaurs and mammals 230 mya

JURASSIC

TRIASSIC

N

EARLY CRETACEOUS

▲ The Mesozoic era is also known as the Age of Dinosaurs. It lasted from 250 to 65 million years ago and includes the Triassic, Jurassic and Cretaceous periods.

Plate tectonics

In the 1960s, geologists found evidence of how the oceans have opened up in the last 200 million years. Seabed rocks are oldest near the coasts and newer in the middle of the oceans. That's because new rocks are formed from magma, molten rock that pushes up through the crust from the mantle. The magma moves slowly upwards and sideways, pulling the oceanic and continental plates apart.

The continental plates move apart

The mid-ocean ridge opens up

The crust

Magma pushes up from the mantle, the thick layer of molten rock between the crust and the core of the Earth.

Late Triassic New Mexico

In 1947, palaeontologists from the American Museum of Natural History came across a big dinosaur site at Ghost Ranch in New Mexico. They dug out hundreds of skeletons of *Coelophysis* from the Late Triassic period 220 million years ago. Since then, other teams have found many more – so many that it has taken nearly 50 years to study them all.

▶ **A large herd of *Coelophysis* was travelling across the dry plains when they were washed away in a flash flood. Their carcasses piled up on a sandbank.**

The fossils

Each slab of rock from Ghost Ranch contained several human-sized skeletons of *Coelophysis*, all tangled up together. The bones came from young and old animals. One or two of the adults had the remains of young *Coelophysis* in their stomachs – not because they were pregnant, but because they were cannibals!

The Late Triassic, when deserts covered many parts of the world, was when the dinosaurs first appeared. The first ones included examples of both main groups: *Eoraptor*, *Coelophysis* and *Plateosaurus* were saurischians; *Pisanosaurus* from Argentina was an ornithischian.

▲ Ned Colbert (left) led the Ghost Ranch team of bone collectors. He continued to work on the site for years, and finally completed his studies of the huge collection of skeletons in 1991.

Colbert is one of the best-known North American dinosaur hunters. He has worked for over 60 years, collecting dinosaurs and other fossils in every continent around the world, even in Antarctica.

Early Jurassic China

Lufengosaurus was the first dinosaur to be excavated and put on display in China – the first finds were made in the 1930s in the Lufeng Formation of the Yunnan Province, and the government proudly issued *Lufengosaurus* stamps. After that, the Chinese palaeontologist C C Young dug up dozens of other dinosaur skeletons. He also trained young palaeontologists to carry on with his work.

Plant-eating teeth

The skull of *Lufengosaurus* shows its relatively small, peg-like teeth. These were good for nipping soft leaves, but no use for chewing. Like most other dinosaurs, *Lufengosaurus* swallowed its food whole, without chewing.

▶ **Two long-necked *Lufengosaurus* crash through the forest. Each animal ate half a tonne of leaves a day – a herd would soon clear all the plant food in the area.**

▲ China is still uncovering a rich heritage of dinosaurs. Fossils of a giant sauropod dating back 150 million years were found near Zigong City in south-west China's Sichuan Province in 1996. The well-preserved remains show that the dinosaur was at least 20 metres long, and had a long neck and tail. It has not been given a name yet.

Lufengosaurus

Massospondylus

Plateosaurus

Lufengosaurus and other prosauropods were the main plant-eaters for nearly 50 million years, during the Late Triassic and Early Jurassic. At that time, they were the biggest land animals that had ever lived. They moved slowly on all fours, but could rear up on their hindlegs to reach leaves on a tall tree.

▲ Prosauropods from different parts of the world – *Lufengosaurus* from China, *Massospondylus* from South Africa and *Plateosaurus* from Germany – were very similar. They were 5 to 10 metres long, and all had long necks and tails, bulky bodies, and strong arms and legs.

▶ *Cetiosaurus* was one of the first sauropods, and it still had some primitive features. For example, its vertebrae were solid. Late Jurassic sauropods had air spaces to save weight.

▼ *Lexovisaurus* was a stegosaur, or 'plated' dinosaur, similar to its more famous relative *Stegosaurus* from the Late Jurassic, but with slender spikes along its back.

Middle Jurassic England

In the Middle Jurassic period, Oxfordshire was on a tropical shoreline. Giant plant-eating sauropods such as *Cetiosaurus* barged through the sparse woodlands. The first big flesh-eating dinosaur, *Megalosaurus*, was stalking its next meal, *Lexovisaurus*.

▲ The sauropods were quite the biggest dinosaurs of all time. Mid-Jurassic Oxford also had smaller animals such as salamanders and lizards.

Naming a dinosaur

Megalosaurus had a jawbone lined with many large sharp teeth. As in all flesh-eating dinosaurs, the teeth curved backwards. This helped the dinosaur hang on to its prey and stopped the prey from struggling free. This piece of jaw is the type specimen – in other words it is the original specimen that was first given the name *Megalosaurus*. It can still be seen in the Oxford University museum.

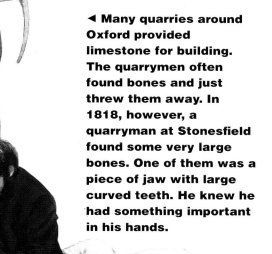

◄ Many quarries around Oxford provided limestone for building. The quarrymen often found bones and just threw them away. In 1818, however, a quarryman at Stonesfield found some very large bones. One of them was a piece of jaw with large curved teeth. He knew he had something important in his hands.

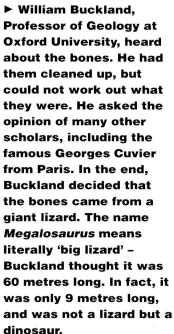

► William Buckland, Professor of Geology at Oxford University, heard about the bones. He had them cleaned up, but could not work out what they were. He asked the opinion of many other scholars, including the famous Georges Cuvier from Paris. In the end, Buckland decided that the bones came from a giant lizard. The name *Megalosaurus* means literally 'big lizard' – Buckland thought it was 60 metres long. In fact, it was only 9 metres long, and was not a lizard but a dinosaur.

When the first dinosaur bone was dug up in 1676 near Oxford, scientists thought it came from a giant human or an elephant. The 1818 discovery of *Megalosaurus* in the same area marked the beginning of serious dinosaur studies. *Megalosaurus* was the first dinosaur ever to be named, in 1824. *Cetiosaurus* was the first sauropod dinosaur to be named, in 1842.

Early Cretaceous North Africa

North Africa 120 million years ago was a lush tropical landscape that teemed with life. Today, dinosaur fossils are found in dry, lifeless desert areas. New discoveries from Niger, in the Sahara region, include the flesh-eating dinosaur *Afrovenator*. Its closest relative seems to be *Allosaurus* from North America.

▼ The flesh-eater *Afrovenator* lived side by side with other dinosaurs and crocodiles. It was 9 to 10 metres long, and fed on plant-eating dinosaurs and other, smaller animals.

Primitive trees and seed ferns grew in the swamp forests of Niger. The ponds and lakes were filled with thick-scaled fishes, which were preyed on by crocodiles. The scene was like Early Cretaceous Europe in some ways, but with different species of dinosaurs. These show that the African continent had partly moved away from the rest of the world by that time.

▶ The palaeontologist Paul Sereno named *Afrovenator* in 1995. It had taken him a long time to gain access to the Niger site. Then he had spent many unsuccessful weeks hunting for fossils. Just before it was time to return home, his luck turned – he finally found the skull and part of the skeleton.

▶ In Early Cretaceous Europe the commonest dinosaurs were ornithopods, two-legged plant-eaters such as *Iguanodon* and *Hypsilophodon*. There were some sauropods and large flesh-eaters, but these were rarer in Europe than in Africa at that time.

Iguanodon

Hypsilophodon

Reconstruction

In 1853, Richard Owen made a famous model of *Iguanodon* on all fours, like a rhinoceros. Scientists now think *Iguanodon* could rear up on its hindlegs to feed or to run, balancing its body with a long stiff tail. But it did also walk on all fours, supporting its weight at the front with its arms.

Late Cretaceous Mongolia

The dinosaurs died out 65 million years ago. The very last dinosaurs were some of the most varied and extraordinary, and include some of the best known – giant tyrannosaurs, horned ceratopsians, honking duckbills and terrifying raptors.

▲ The Gobi Desert site produced spectacular finds of dinosaur nests and eggs, belonging to *Protoceratops*. The nests consisted of up to 20 eggs laid upright in layered circles.

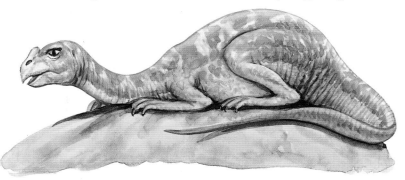

▲ In the 1920s, fossils of a dinosaur were found near a nest. Palaeontologists named it *Oviraptor*, which means 'egg stealer'. But new finds in the 1990s suggest this was a mother *Oviraptor* guarding her own eggs.

Late Cretaceous Mongolia is one of the most exciting dinosaur worlds to explore. Dinosaur bones were first found in the desolate Gobi Desert of Mongolia by an American expedition in the 1920s. Since then, scientists from Russia, Poland and Mongolia have collected fossils there. In the 1990s, new American expeditions have turned up even more spectacular treasures.

▲ Although *Protoceratops* was a little 'horn-faced' ceratopsian, it did not have real horns like its later relative, *Triceratops*. *Saurolophus* had a duckbill like the North American hadrosaurs.

▶ The flesh-eating *Velociraptor* was only two metres long, but it was an intelligent and fast hunter. It has seized a small mammal called *Zalambdalestes*, which was about to raid its nest.

▼ The plant-eating dinosaurs were preyed on by the massive carnivore *Tarbosaurus*, which was up to 12 metres long.

DINOSAURS IN CLOSE-UP

The dinosaurs died out some 60 million years before the first humans appeared.

This makes it difficult to work out how they lived. The closest living relatives of dinosaurs are birds, but it's not much use studying a sparrow to understand how *Tyrannosaurus rex* functioned! So palaeontologists also look at living reptiles such as crocodiles, and at mammals. And they test ideas about dinosaurs' behaviour by looking at fossil evidence of their anatomy.

▲ Some scientists think the giant sauropods could rear up on their hindlegs to reach high leaves. Others say no, their body weight would break their hindlegs and tail.

Their small brain cases indicate a small brain – too small to control such a huge body? Perhaps another nervous centre in the hip area controlled the back half of the body.

The framework

Dinosaurs were vertebrates – they had a backbone. This key structure joined up the whole skeleton. It also contained the spinal cord, which linked the brain to the nerves running all round the body.

Fossilized bones show marks where muscles were attached and blood vessels ran. But no soft internal organs had ever been found – until 1998. Then two exciting new dinosaur specimens were announced, from Italy and China, with all their guts preserved.

tail vertebrae

anus

Movement

T rex was a biped, walking on its massive, muscular hindlegs – its arms were too small to be of any use. *T rex* could probably run as fast as a racehorse (about 50 kilometres per hour), but only for a short distance. Its long tail acted as a counterweight.

Dinosaur skin is rarely preserved. Usually all we have are impressions, marks left by the skin in sand or mud and fossilized. Impressions show whether the skin was scaly or knobbly, but not its colour.

▲ These vertebrae are part of the world's biggest and most complete *Tyrannosaurus* skeleton ever. Discovered in South Dakota, USA in 1991 and nick-named Sue, this ten-tonne dinosaur was sold to a Chicago museum for $8 million (£5.3 million).

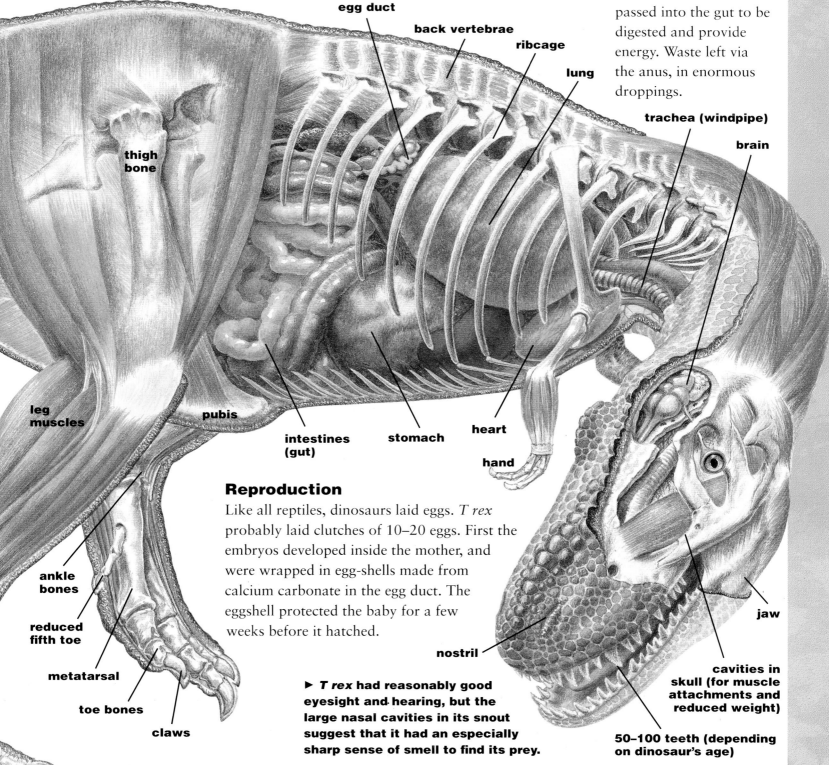

The control centre

T rex's huge bony skull protected its brain and its sense organs – the eyes, ears, tongue and nose. As in other reptiles, the brain case was a tiny box deep inside the skull, like a matchbox in a shoebox.

Circulation

Your heart is the size of your fist. *T rex* needed a heart the size of a pig to pump blood round its massive body – remember, *T rex* stood 6 metres tall and measured 15 metres from nose to tail.

Respiration

All animals need oxygen that comes from the air they breathe. The lungs inside your ribcage are like bellows, expanding as they suck air in and collapsing as the used air is pushed out. *T rex* had a pair of lungs the size of a car.

Digestion

T rex was a carnivore and tore up meat with sharp teeth that were 18 centimetres long. Inside its stomach, which was 3 to 4 metres wide, food was ground into a fine paste with the help of stomach stones. Then it passed into the gut to be digested and provide energy. Waste left via the anus, in enormous droppings.

egg duct

back vertebrae

ribcage

lung

trachea (windpipe)

brain

thigh bone

leg muscles

pubis

intestines (gut)

stomach

heart

hand

Reproduction

Like all reptiles, dinosaurs laid eggs. *T rex* probably laid clutches of 10–20 eggs. First the embryos developed inside the mother, and were wrapped in egg-shells made from calcium carbonate in the egg duct. The eggshell protected the baby for a few weeks before it hatched.

ankle bones

reduced fifth toe

metatarsal

toe bones

claws

nostril

jaw

cavities in skull (for muscle attachments and reduced weight)

► **T rex had reasonably good eyesight and hearing, but the large nasal cavities in its snout suggest that it had an especially sharp sense of smell to find its prey.**

50–100 teeth (depending on dinosaur's age)

Male and female

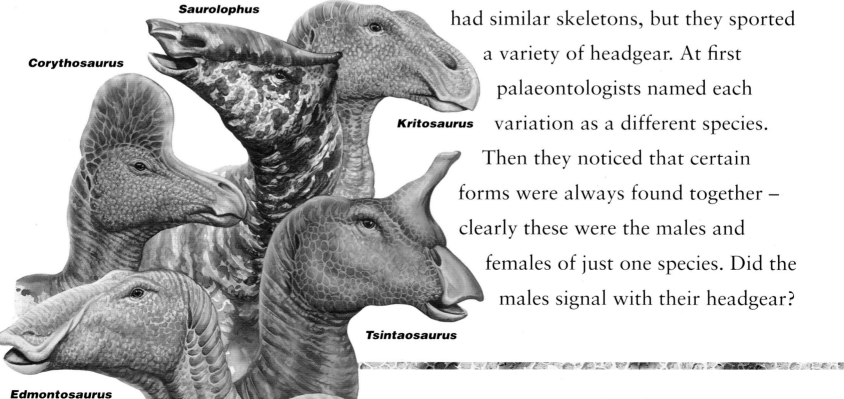

With some animals, it is easy to identify males and females, especially when the two sexes signal to each other with special colours, crests or cries. How can we tell with dinosaurs? Fossils show that some males were bigger than females, or had longer horns. But scientists have to speculate about other differences by comparing dinosaurs with modern animals.

▼ Some hadrosaurs, such as *Corythosaurus* and *Tsintaosaurus*, had bony crests that were probably covered with bright-coloured skin. Other hadrosaurs, such as *Saurolophus, Kritosaurus* and *Edmontosaurus*, could blow up balloon-like airsacs over the nose to show off to females or scare off rivals – like the lizards and snakes that expand the skin over the throat or behind the head.

The hadrosaurs, or duck-billed dinosaurs, show clear distinctions between males and females. They all had similar skeletons, but they sported a variety of headgear. At first palaeontologists named each variation as a different species. Then they noticed that certain forms were always found together – clearly these were the males and females of just one species. Did the males signal with their headgear?

Saurolophus

Corythosaurus

Kritosaurus

Tsintaosaurus

Edmontosaurus

▼ In this herd of hadrosaurs, a female *Parasaurolophus* on the right stands guard over her young. Two males on the left are having a small tiff about who is boss. Another male scents danger and cries out an alarm to warn the herd.

◄ *Parasaurolophus* had a long tubular crest over the back of its head. This was made from the snout bones – the air passages ran up from the nostrils through the crest and down to the throat. As *Parasaurolophus* breathed in and out, it could make hooting and honking sounds.

The sounds were different for each crest size and shape, so males, females and juveniles each had their own call. Recently, scientists have made models of different hadrosaur skulls. When they blew through them, they found that different crests gave different sounds, just like the different instruments in a brass band.

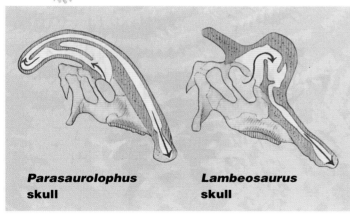

Parasaurolophus skull

Lambeosaurus skull

Air flow

When you cut through a hadrosaur skull, you can see how the air flowed up through the crest as the animal breathed. The coils and twists in the air passages are like the complex shapes of a trumpet.

Fighting

Cretaceous landscapes echoed to the sound of male hadrosaurs honking and hooting at each other, and to the crash of pachycephalosaur skulls. Modern animals fight for a variety of reasons. As well as fighting with predators to protect themselves, the males fight to establish which one will be leader of the herd. Many dinosaurs probably did the same.

▲ The pachycephalosaurs had extra-thick and bony skull roofs. Perhaps the males battled with each other in head-butting contests. Mountain sheep and deer crash heads like this to establish dominance over the herd.

Birth and death

Palaeontologists know more about the birth of dinosaurs than about their death. Hundreds of fossil eggs have been found. They had hard limy shells, just like bird's eggs, and were laid in clutches of 10 to 40.

Egg Mountain

Maiasaura, a hadrosaur from the Late Cretaceous period, made nests in colonies. In 1984 over 20 nests were found at Egg Mountain in Montana, USA. The mothers made nests by scraping a hollow in the ground. They laid about 20 eggs, then covered them with sand and vegetation to keep them warm. After 3 to 4 weeks, the babies hatched – they had a sharp little tooth on their snout to break through the hard eggshell. Perhaps the parents, or older brothers and sisters, stayed around to guard against egg-stealers such as *Troodon*.

▶ When the *Maiasaura* babies hatched, their mother brought them succulent plant shoots to eat. After a few weeks they could wander off and forage for themselves. But the family group probably kept together for safety.

▶ Dinosaur eggs were all kinds of different shapes, some of them round like large bird's eggs, others long and sausage-shaped. Some remarkable fossil eggs found in North America and China in the 1990s show the tiny bones of embryo dinosaurs inside. These eggs must have been covered by sand before the babies could hatch.

embryo inside an egg

ceratopsian, 10–40 cm long, 15–30 per clutch

sauropod, 30–90 cm long, 8–12 per clutch

hadrosaur, 10–40 cm long, 15–30 per clutch

Growing up

A remarkable series of fossils shows how *Maiasaura* grew up. The tiny hatchlings had short snouts and their duckbills had barely begun to develop. They were born with a full set of teeth, so they were ready to eat plants right away. As they grew bigger, the snout lengthened and broadened.

hatchling

young *Maiasaura*

adult *Maiasaura*

Why did dinosaurs not lay big eggs? In scale with a hen, an *Apatosaurus* egg should have been the size of a car. But the biggest dinosaur egg, laid by the sauropod *Hypselosaurus*, is less than one metre long, and most were much smaller. The reason for this is that the thickness of an eggshell is proportional to the volume of the egg. If an egg's volume is more than ten litres, the shell is so thick that the baby cannot break out.

Old bones

There is no clear evidence about dinosaur age – the large ones probably lived for a hundred years or more. We do know about dinosaur disease, though. Dinosaurs suffered from arthritis, gout, rheumatism and other diseases that made their bones seize up.

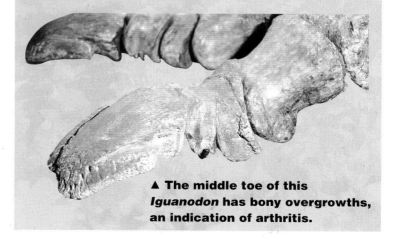

▲ The middle toe of this *Iguanodon* has bony overgrowths, an indication of arthritis.

On the move

Dinosaur herds sometimes travelled huge distances. They migrated hundreds of miles in search of food, or to escape the colder winter weather. The big plant-eaters moved to new feeding grounds when they had stripped all the leaves from the trees.

▶ A herd of *Saltasaurus* on the move in Argentina 100 million years ago. These huge sauropods probably lived in herds of 10 to 20 animals. When they set off to find fresh food, the adults probably walked on the outside with the young in the middle, for safety.

Palaeontologists know about dinosaur movements from their footprints, which are preserved in hundreds of sites around the world. The first dinosaur tracks, made by small theropods such as *Coelophysis*, were found in North America 200 years ago by a schoolboy.

► The American palaeontologist Scott Madsen exposes Early Jurassic tracks at the Moenave Formation in the Painted Desert, Arizona. These three-toed footprints were made by two or three species of theropods, the two-legged flesh-eating dinosaurs. Each species had a different size and shape of foot.

How fast?

Palaeontologists can work out how fast dinosaurs ran from the length of their stride and the length of their leg. The faster the animal is moving, the longer its stride length. This works for two-legged and four-legged dinosaurs.

leg length

Key:
front footprint
back footprint

stride length

The first dinosaur tracks were thought to have been made by giant birds. This was because many dinosaur footprints have three long toes. Larger dinosaurs such as the sauropods made more stump-like footprints, with four or five short toes. Footprints are matched to dinosaurs by comparing the size and shape of their footbones.

Triceratops

Apatosaurus

Hypsilophodon

Tyrannosaurus

Triceratops trotted at about 16 to 24 kilometres per hour, like a rhinoceros. This was fast enough to charge at an attacker and frighten it off.

The 40-tonne **Apatosaurus** ambled along at 8 to 16 kilometres per hour. If it had tried to run, the 400-tonne impact would have shattered its leg bones.

Hypsilophodon was small, just 2 metres long. At first palaeontologists thought it lived in trees – in fact it ran along the ground at up to 50 kilometres per hour.

A 10-tonne **Tyrannosaurus** walked at 16 kilometres per hour. Some scientists think it could also run a lot faster, but it was probably too heavy to run for long.

Eating plants

Most dinosaurs were herbivores, or plant-eaters, yet plants are stringy or woody and hard to digest. To get enough energy from this food, *Iguanodon* had to spend most of the day eating. It consumed huge amounts of leaves, grinding them between 100 teeth by moving the upper jaw sideways.

Heterodontosaurus (1) had narrow teeth for chewing. *Plateosaurus* (2), *Diplodocus* (3) and *Apatosaurus* (4) crushed food with peg-like teeth. *Stegosaurus* (5) had broad ridged teeth for slicing.

▼ *Iguanodon* seized mouthfuls of leaves with its long tongue, like a giraffe, and nipped them off with its hard beak.

Stomach stones, or gastroliths, have been found in the ribcages of several dinosaurs. When these pebbles were swallowed, they tumbled and crunched in the stomach, breaking up the plant food. Hens eat grit to do the same thing.

Plants

Grass did not appear until long after the dinosaurs died out. Herbivorous dinosaurs fed on low bushy plants such as ferns, horsetails, ginkgos and cycads. They also ate the tough, primitive conifers and some of the flowering plants that grew at that time. We know this from plant fossils, usually flattened, black leaf shapes in the rock.

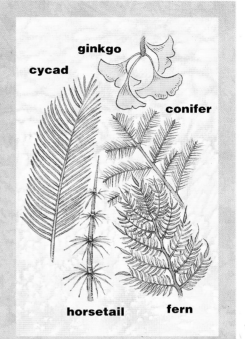

How much did they eat?

Brachiosaurus was one of the biggest sauropods, weighing about 80 tonnes. An elephant weighs about 5 tonnes and eats about 50 kilograms of plant material in a day. So did *Brachiosaurus* eat 800 kg a day? Probably not.

How could it have packed that much food into its tiny mouth and down its narrow neck? It probably ate less than 400 kg a day.

Herbivorous dinosaurs were not very efficient at processing plant food. Most of them could not move their jaws from side to side to chew, so they swallowed leaves and branches whole. Some dinosaurs had stomach stones to to help grind the food in their stomach. Others had microbes inside the stomach to help digest woody plant material. No doubt this produced a great deal of gas before waste was passed out in the form of huge droppings. Fossilized droppings are called coprolites.

The biggest coprolites, from flesh-eaters like *T rex*, are 50 cm long.

35

Killing claw

Deinonychus was armed with a curved, scythe-like claw on the second toe of its foot. While the dinosaur was running, the claw was held off the ground to keep it sharp. At the kill, *Deinonychus* could swing the claw through its prey and make a deep cut one metre long or more.

► Small dinosaurs such as *Deinonychus* hunted in packs, just as hunting dogs do today. Five or six of them chased their prey, maybe for several kilometres, nipping at its heels and tearing its flesh. Eventually the large herbivore fell to the ground, utterly exhausted. That's when the pack moved in for the kill.

Hunting and scavenging

The theropod dinosaurs were the only flesh-eaters, or carnivores. Some were scavengers and fed on animals that were already dead. Others were active hunters that chased and killed their own prey, ranging from insects to other dinosaurs.

► *Tyrannosaurus, Allosaurus* and *Dilophosaurus* had long, curved teeth for ripping into big plant-eaters. *Troodon* and *Harpymimus* had tiny teeth for cutting up smaller prey. *Avimimus* and *Oviraptor* had no teeth, but they could crush eggs or bugs with their strong, beak-like jaws.

Tyrannosaurus

Allosaurus

Troodon

Avimimus

Oviraptor

Dilophosaurus

Harpymimus

▶ This famous fossil, found by a team of Polish scientists in the 1960s, shows a carnivore making a kill. *Velociraptor* (on the right) was a close relative of *Deinonychus*. It has hooked its claws under the jaw of the small horn-faced dinosaur *Protoceratops*. While they were fighting, the two dinosaurs were buried in a sand-storm and suffocated.

Palaeontologists usually have to guess how carnivores hunted their prey, but not with *Deinonychus*. Sites in Montana and Wyoming, USA, each show that a *Tenontosaurus* and several *Deinonychus* died together after a struggle. Scattered *Deinonychus* teeth show that this pack of small carnivores had been biting at the larger plant-eater.

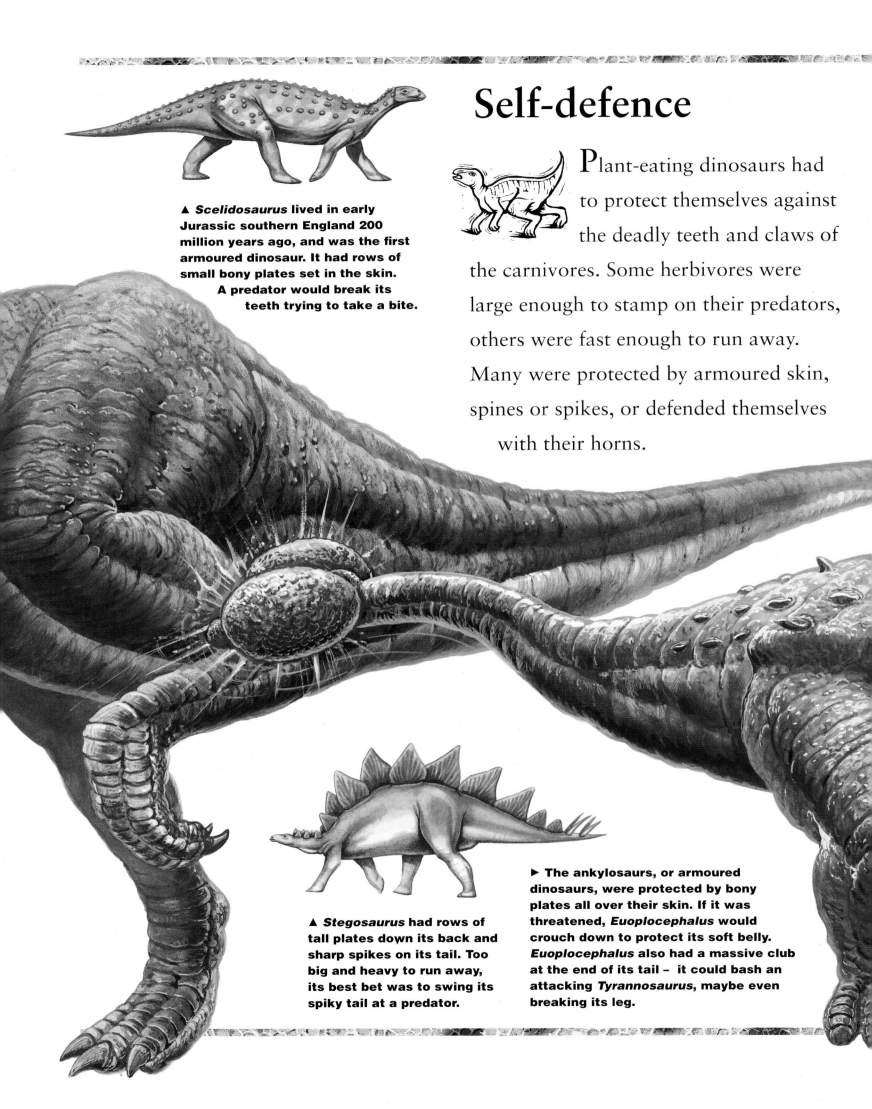

Self-defence

▲ *Scelidosaurus* lived in early Jurassic southern England 200 million years ago, and was the first armoured dinosaur. It had rows of small bony plates set in the skin. A predator would break its teeth trying to take a bite.

Plant-eating dinosaurs had to protect themselves against the deadly teeth and claws of the carnivores. Some herbivores were large enough to stamp on their predators, others were fast enough to run away. Many were protected by armoured skin, spines or spikes, or defended themselves with their horns.

▲ *Stegosaurus* had rows of tall plates down its back and sharp spikes on its tail. Too big and heavy to run away, its best bet was to swing its spiky tail at a predator.

► The ankylosaurs, or armoured dinosaurs, were protected by bony plates all over their skin. If it was threatened, *Euoplocephalus* would crouch down to protect its soft belly. *Euoplocephalus* also had a massive club at the end of its tail – it could bash an attacking *Tyrannosaurus*, maybe even breaking its leg.

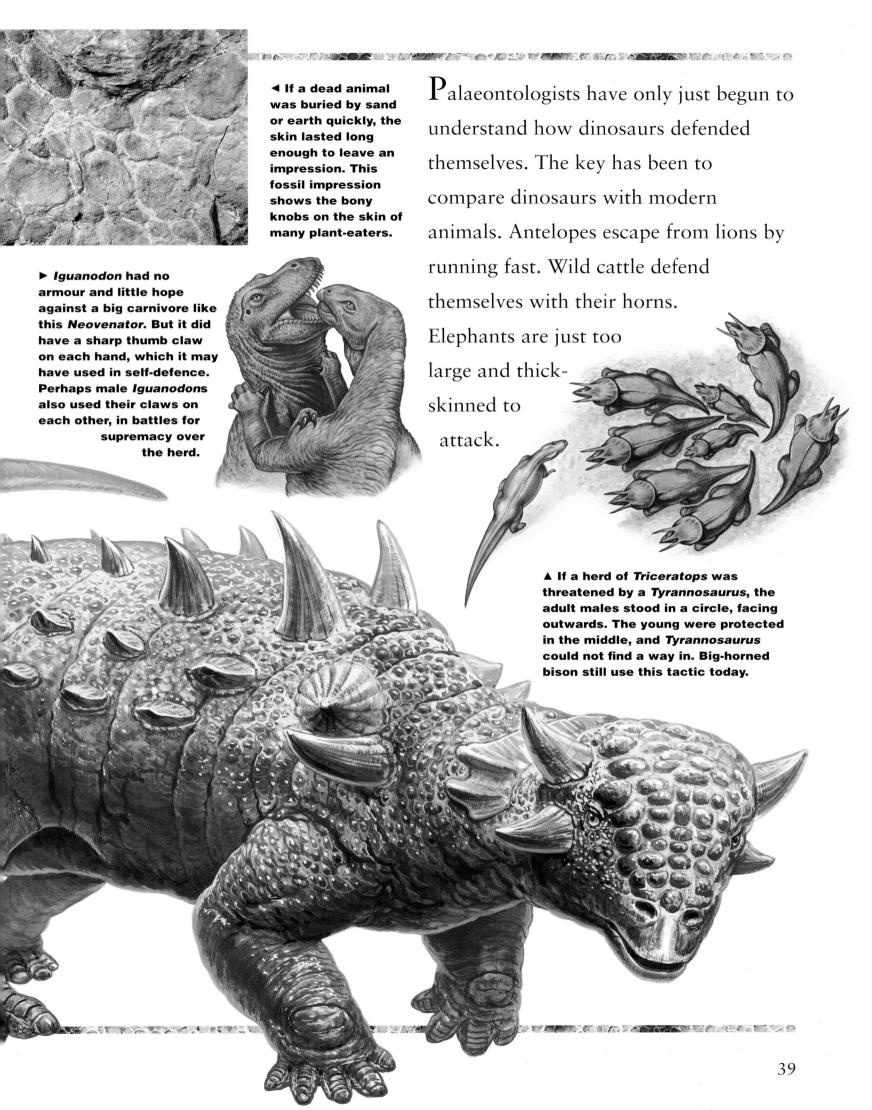

◄ If a dead animal was buried by sand or earth quickly, the skin lasted long enough to leave an impression. This fossil impression shows the bony knobs on the skin of many plant-eaters.

► *Iguanodon* had no armour and little hope against a big carnivore like this *Neovenator*. But it did have a sharp thumb claw on each hand, which it may have used in self-defence. Perhaps male *Iguanodon*s also used their claws on each other, in battles for supremacy over the herd.

Palaeontologists have only just begun to understand how dinosaurs defended themselves. The key has been to compare dinosaurs with modern animals. Antelopes escape from lions by running fast. Wild cattle defend themselves with their horns. Elephants are just too large and thick-skinned to attack.

▲ If a herd of *Triceratops* was threatened by a *Tyrannosaurus*, the adult males stood in a circle, facing outwards. The young were protected in the middle, and *Tyrannosaurus* could not find a way in. Big-horned bison still use this tactic today.

39

Cold-blooded?

Were dinosaurs warm-blooded like birds and mammals, using food energy to keep themselves warm? Or were they cold-blooded like modern reptiles, which bask in the sun but cannot control their body temperature? There is still no final answer, but it seems that dinosaurs were somewhere in between.

Fast or slow?

A warm-blooded dinosaur would have moved faster than a cold-blooded one. So did *Tyrannosaurus* chase after its prey, or did it feed more passively, scavenging on animals that had died by accident or from old age?

▶ In the Cretaceous period Australia was close to the freezing South Pole. Yet this large iguanodontid *Muttaburrasaurus* lived there, and at Dinosaur Cove fossils have been found for *Leaellynasaura*, a small ornithopod.

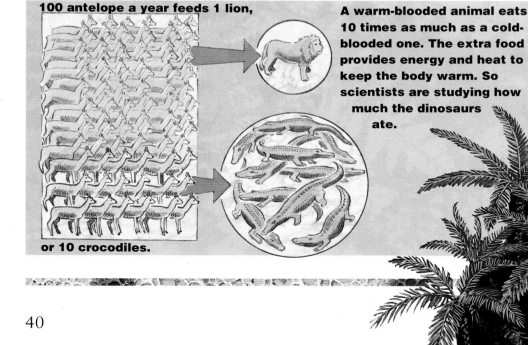

100 antelope a year feeds 1 lion,

or 10 crocodiles.

A warm-blooded animal eats 10 times as much as a cold-blooded one. The extra food provides energy and heat to keep the body warm. So scientists are studying how much the dinosaurs ate.

Dinosaurs have been found near the North and South Poles. Palaeontologists suggested this proved the dinosaurs were warm-blooded, or how else could they have survived the cold and snow? But we now believe that the larger dinosaurs were cold-blooded. Because they were so big, their body temperature stayed fairly constant even in the cold. Some smaller carnivores may have been warm-blooded.

Recent research shows that, under the microscope, some bones have the warm-blooded feature of holes (at the top of this photo), showing continuous growth. Other bones have the cold-blooded feature of seasonal growth rings (the bands at the bottom of this photo), stopping in the winter, starting again in the summer. How can one dinosaur have both?

What the nose shows

Mammals and birds have thin sheets of bone covered with moist skin inside their noses. These turbinates cut down loss of heat while the animal breathes out. Cold-blooded animals do not have turbinates, since they do not control body temperature very closely. In 1995, it was found that dinosaurs did not have turbinates either. The debate continues!

turbinates

a dog's skull

DINOSAUR NEIGHBOURS

Dinosaurs were the most successful of all land animals, dominating the world for 140 million years. But as the Cretaceous period advanced, they had to compete with other creatures that shared their habitat. Small mammals flourished, and winged creatures took to the air – ranging from the world's first tiny moths and bees to large dragonflies and the first birds. Some of these species would outlast the dinosaurs.

early mammal

fern

dragonfly

tortoise

Hypsilophodon

▶ All kinds of insects are preserved in amber, the fossilized resin that was once the sticky sap of trees. Often the insects have all their legs, wings and feelers. Some even show their colour patterns. New fossil finds are made all the time. In 1998, the oldest known ants, 92 million years old, were reported in New Jersey, USA.

▶ In the Wealden of south-east England 125 million years ago, large crocodiles and turtles swam in the rivers, midges swarmed, and pterosaurs dominated the sky. Horsetails, ferns, conifers and the first flowering plants grew in abundance.

pterosaur

early
birds

Ornithocheirus

conifers

Baryonyx
('Heavy Claw')

fish

Iguanodon

horsetails

frog

43

Any survivors?

Of the three groups of marine reptiles shown here, only the turtles are still around. The long-necked plesiosaurs were a fourth group – legend has it that one has survived, a descendent of plesiosaurs trapped in Loch Ness when the seas receded millions of years ago...

► **Archelon** was a large sea turtle with a shell 3 metres long. It used its huge front paddles to 'fly' underwater, beating them up and down like the wings of a bird. It probably reached speeds of 10 to 15 kilometres per hour.

► **Mosasaurs** hunted fishes and shellfish during the Late Cretaceous. *Platecarpus* was over 4 metres long, and more like a big dolphin than a lizard. It swam by beating its tail from side to side. The paddles were used only for steering.

▲ *Ichthyosaurus* also swam by beating its tail from side to side. Ichthyosaurs date from the start of the Mesozoic era, and flourished in seas all round the world by the Jurassic. They ranged in size from 1 to 10 metres. Like dolphins and other sea mammals, these reptiles bore live young at sea.

She sells seashells

This tongue-twister comes from a rhyme about Mary Anning, a famous fossil dealer. Early in the 19th century, she found some skeletons of ichthyosaurs and plesiosaurs on the shore at Lyme Regis in Dorset. These were the first finds of giant Mesozoic marine reptiles, and she sold them at high prices.

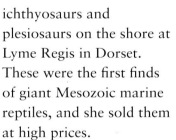

In the sea...

Dinosaurs were not the only large reptiles of the Mesozoic era. A whole range of marine reptiles swam in the seas, hunting fishes and one another. The biggest mosasaurs and plesiosaurs were over ten metres long, the size of a killer whale. They all died out 65 million years ago – except the turtles, which survive to this day.

... and in the air

Animals took to the air during the age of the dinosaurs. Most successful were the pterosaurs, which were winged reptiles and were not related to birds. They lived side by side with the dinosaurs for 165 million years.

▼ A pterosaur's wings were made from leathery skin. They stretched out behind a long bony strut made from the bone of each arm, plus an enormously elongated fourth finger that reached right to the pointed wing tip. Their long thin wings, like those of a seagull or an albatross, were the best shape for soaring.

They used the rising air in front of the cliffs for lift and then they could glide for long distances with only a few flaps from time to time.

▲ Some of the most spectacular pterosaur fossils come from the Solnhofen limestones of southern Germany. Some, such as *Rhamphorhynchus*, had a long tail that was used for steering. Others, such as *Pterodactylus*, had only a short tail.

How big were they?

For a time, *Pteranodon* was the record holder, with a wingspan of 7 metres. In the 1970s an even bigger pterosaur, *Quetzalcoatlus*, was found in Texas, USA. Its wingspan was an amazing 12 to 14 metres wide. That's even bigger than a hang glider.

Quetzalcoatlus

Pteranodon

Ornithocheirus
Rhamphorhynchus

Birds and mammals

Birds and mammals lived side by side with the dinosaurs. The best-known evidence for this comes from *Archaeopteryx*, the first bird, which was discovered in Solnhofen in southern Germany. *Archaeopteryx* fossils are rare and very valuable – only seven have been found so far.

The first *Archaeopteryx* fossil to be found, in 1860, was a single feather. The latest, in 1992, was a complete skeleton with wing and tail feathers.

From dinosaurs to birds

Most palaeontologists think that birds evolved from small theropods such as *Compsognathus*, a dinosaur with long arms but no wings and almost certainly no feathers. *Archaeopteryx* is often said to be a 'missing link'. It had feathers and wings, so it was clearly a bird. However, it still had the teeth, finger claws and long bony tail of a reptile, whereas modern birds have lost those features.

Compsognathus skeleton

Archaeopteryx skeleton

Modern bird's skeleton

▶ Early mammals such as *Zalambdalestes* and *Deltatheridium* were small shrew-like animals that may have lived in burrows, safe from the dinosaurs. They used their powerful sense of smell to find bugs and worms.

The first mammals

The first mammals lived at the same time as the first dinosaurs, but their tiny fossils are very rare. They evolved from mammal-like reptiles in the Late Triassic, some 225 million years ago. But the dinosaurs were bigger, and while they dominated the Earth the mammals could not flourish.

Unlike the dinosaurs, mammals are highly successful today. They are covered in hair and they are warm-blooded, which allows them to hunt at night and to live in cold conditions. Mammals are also more intelligent than reptiles. They care for their young for longer than most other animals, and feed them on their own milk. Different mammals have different teeth, and this is a clue to their great success – as a group, they can feed on a huge range of foods.

Zalambdalestes skull

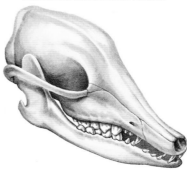

Megazostrodon skull

Skulls and teeth

Early mammals such as *Zalambdalestes* and *Megazostrodon* had a large brain that filled the back of the skull – unlike the skull of a reptile, which has a tiny braincase tucked well inside. The mammals also had small sharp teeth for piercing insects. Further back they had broad teeth for grinding and crushing their food. That meant better digestion and more energy for brain and body.

THE END

A skeleton at Hell Creek, Montana, USA, is all that's left of a *Tyrannosaurus*. Even now, 65 million years later, the extinction of the dinosaurs is one of the great unsolved mysteries. Why did such a big, successful group of animals disappear? Hundreds of scientists have studied the question. Perhaps a giant meteorite hit the Earth and vast dust clouds and bitter cold killed the dinosaurs. Perhaps they died out over a longer period, after long-term changes to the climate. There may be more than one explanation...

◄ Early theories about the extinction of the dinosaurs concentrated on the other animals and plants of the time. Perhaps the mammals ate up all the dinosaur eggs, or the new flowering plants were poisonous? Perhaps the dinosaurs were stupid enough to run into trees, or grew too heavy and suffered from slipped discs? These ideas are fun, but unlikely.

How long did it take?

Did the dinosaurs decline over millions of years, or did they die out overnight? Studies show that they disappeared gradually in some places, but more abruptly in others. Other animals that disappeared included the pterosaurs, marine reptiles and some other sea creatures. Any extinction theory must take account of the fact that most other plants and animals survived.

Climate change

During the Late Cretaceous period, the climate in North America became cooler and more seasonal. This is shown by major changes in the plants – tropical plants vanished and cool-climate plants replaced them. The dinosaurs seem to have moved further and further south, and warm-blooded mammals replaced them in the new cool-climate conifer forests.

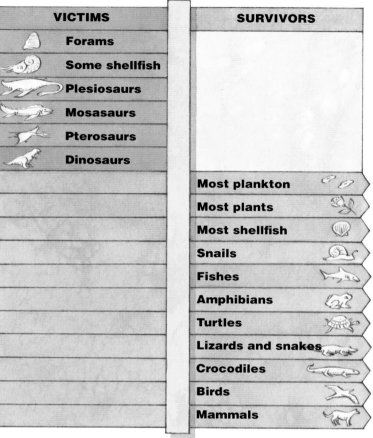

VICTIMS	SURVIVORS
Forams	
Some shellfish	
Plesiosaurs	
Mosasaurs	
Pterosaurs	
Dinosaurs	
	Most plankton
	Most plants
	Most shellfish
	Snails
	Fishes
	Amphibians
	Turtles
	Lizards and snakes
	Crocodiles
	Birds
	Mammals

▲ Volcanoes send up dust and gases that can affect the whole Earth. Some of the gases can make the atmosphere much hotter, and others make it much cooler. Shock heating and cooling can kill off life.

Did the dinosaurs die out gradually as a result of changes in the climate? If so, why did the climate become cooler? Perhaps there were huge eruptions of volcanoes over a period of half a million years or more. The evidence for this comes from India, where enormous amounts of lava were poured out in the Deccan region at the end of the Cretaceous period.

► At the end of the Cretaceous and the start of the Tertiary, something dramatic caused fine dust to fall from the sky all over the world, forming a dark clay layer. This layer is called the KT (Cretaceous –Tertiary) boundary, and can be seen here at Zumaya in Spain – between the mudstone at the bottom and the whitish limestone above.

What died out?

Dinosaurs, pterosaurs, plesiosaurs and mosasaurs all died out at the KT boundary. So did swimming shellfish such as ammonites and belemnites, and groups of plankton, the microscopic floating creatures on the surface of the sea. Some of these animals seemed to die out overnight – or at least in the space of only a few years. Why did they disappear and others not? Was it just bad luck?

Fatal impact

The most popular theory for the extinction of the dinosaurs was published by American physicist Luis Alvarez in 1980. He suggested that the Earth was hit by a huge meteorite, ten kilometres across. The impact threw up a huge dust cloud that blanketed the whole world and cut out the sunlight, causing darkness and freezing cold. Plants died because they need sunlight, and animals died because they were frozen to death.

A dense black cloud

A meteorite 10 kilometres wide would make a crater at least 150 kilometres across. This is big enough to throw out millions of tonnes of rocks and dust. The rocks would fall down to Earth around the crater, but the fine dust would be thrown high into the atmosphere, taking many months or even years to fall back. During that time a dense black cloud would cover the whole Earth, cutting out the sunlight.

► When a meteorite hits Earth, the huge force of impact drives it deep into the ground, where the enormously high pressure turns it into vapour. Tonnes of rocks and dust are thrown up into the air and explode outwards.

The explosion kills all life within many kilometres of the impact site, knocking trees sideways and blasting animals with heat and rocks. If the meteorite lands in the sea, tidal waves called tsunamis are set off. When they reach land and crash down from a height of 20 metres or more, they wreak havoc.

After the impact theory was proposed, scientists searched for the crater. Where had the meteorite actually landed? In 1991 came exciting news: there were signs of a huge crater at Chicxulub in southern Mexico, partly on land and partly on the seabed. It was buried deep under rocks deposited in the last 65 million years, but its shape showed up on surveys. Geologists sank boreholes 500 metres deep into the centre of the crater and found evidence of the high temperature and pressure produced when a meteorite hits the Earth's crust.

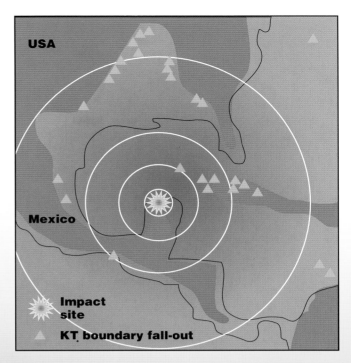

Finding the crater site

In the 1980s, geologists found three sets of clues. First they noticed that the layers of KT boundary fall-out were much thicker around the Caribbean than anywhere else in the world. Then they found some strange rock sequences around the coastline. These contained huge blocks of older rock, dumped there by tsunamis. Finally, in 1991, close study of boreholes pinpointed where the crater lay – Chicxulub, Mexico.

▼ The key evidence for the impact theory was the discovery of iridium at the KT boundary in Italy and Denmark. Iridium is a rare metal that arrives from space in meteorites. It has now been found all over the world, showing that a dust cloud circled the globe, dispersing iridium everywhere. That makes the meteorite a prime suspect for the extinction of the dinosaurs.

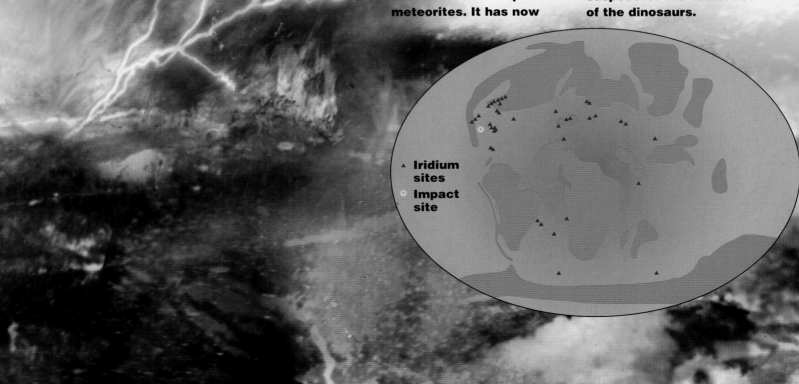

When did dinomania begin?

In 1824, English naturalist William Buckland published the first scientific account of a dinosaur, *Megalosaurus*. The following year, Gideon Mantell described the teeth and bones of *Iguanodon*. In Paris, meanwhile, Georges Cuvier produced life-like reconstructions of extinct animals by matching their skeletons with living species.

◄ Owen and Hawkins' scary models still lurk among the bushes in the grounds of the Crystal Palace exhibition centre in London.

▼ These dinosaur sculptures surprise drivers at a truck stop in Banning, California.

▲ In 1854, fossil hunter Richard Owen and sculptor Waterhouse Hawkins had 20 scientists to dinner inside their life-size model of an *Iguanodon*.

Owen and Hawkins were recreating a whole zoo of prehistoric animals for the Great Exhibition when it moved from Hyde Park to Crystal Palace, London.

Dinosaurs forever!

Sixty-five million years after their extinction, dinosaurs made their come-back. When their bones were first uncovered, people thought they must have belonged to giant humans from biblical times, or to elephants. In 1842, Richard Owen announced that they actually belonged to a group of extinct animals he called Dinosauria ('terrible lizards').

In the news

Following the work of Cuvier, Buckland, Mantell and Owen, dinomania quickly spread across Europe and the United States. Two rival bone collectors, Edward Cope and Othniel Marsh, raced to find new species in the American midwest. The newspapers reported every new find, and museum exhibits attracted huge crowds. By the end of the 19th century, everyone had heard of dinosaurs.

▼ It wasn't long before dinosaurs crossed from science to science fiction. Sir Arthur Conan Doyle's *Lost World* was a bestselling book (1912) and a silent film (1925).

Early exhibitions showed lumbering monsters of little or no intelligence. On the silver screen, clay models wobbled out of the swamp to terrorize the world. Nowadays we know so much about dinosaurs' anatomy and behaviour that they seem as real and complex as modern animals. Films with stunning special effects and record-breaking audiences mean that dinosaurs rule the Earth once more.

► The Flintstones are the world's best-known Stone-Age family. They shot to fame in the 1960s, in a cartoon show on American tv. Their lovable pet, Dino, even had his own weekly comic. Like most of the dinosaurs on this page, Dino is scientifically inaccurate but fun.

◄ A bucking *Triceratops* and his rodeo rider in Drumheller, Canada.

▼ Barney the Dinosaur at Macy's Thanksgiving Day parade in New York.

▼▼ The biggest carnivores ever make a tasty snack.

◄ In *King Kong versus Godzilla* (1962) two of the most popular monsters in science fiction come face to face. King Kong is a giant ape (at least 20 metres tall) rampaging across New York. Godzilla is a dragon-like dinosaur of equally awesome proportions. Created in Japan in 1954, Godzilla rises out of the sea in dozens of films.

An Adventure 65 Million Years In The Making.

JURASSIC PARK

◄ In 1993, the Steven Spielberg film *Jurassic Park* broke box office records. Based on a novel by Michael Crichton, it tells the story of a scientist creating dinosaurs from DNA extracted from a mosquito that had bitten a dinosaur and been preserved in amber. In fact, scientists say this could never happen. But the animatronic and virtual reality dinosaurs that leap across the screen look and sound scarily real!

A to Z of dinosaurs

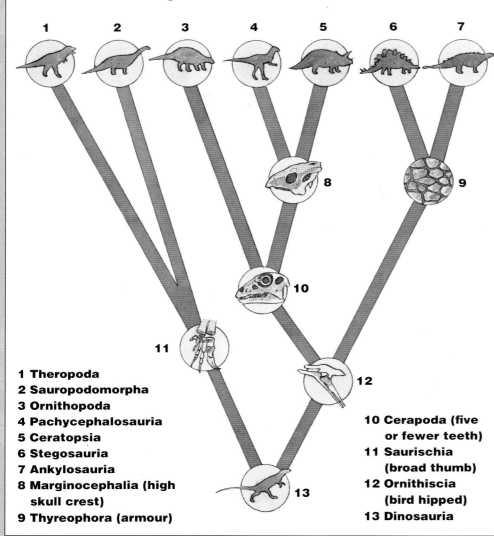

The family tree

The evolutionary tree of dinosaurs shows how the seven main groups are related to one another. After their origin 230 million years ago, dinosaurs split into several groups. The species in each group are recognized by particular shared features of the skull and skeleton.

1 **Theropoda**
2 **Sauropodomorpha**
3 **Ornithopoda**
4 **Pachycephalosauria**
5 **Ceratopsia**
6 **Stegosauria**
7 **Ankylosauria**
8 **Marginocephalia (high skull crest)**
9 **Thyreophora (armour)**
10 **Cerapoda (five or fewer teeth)**
11 **Saurischia (broad thumb)**
12 **Ornithiscia (bird hipped)**
13 **Dinosauria**

Afrovenator A-FRO-VEN-AH-TOR
CLASSIFICATION: Theropoda
WHERE AND WHEN: North Africa; Early Cretaceous
CLOSEST RELATIVES: *Allosaurus, Megalosaurus*
NAMED BY: Paul Sereno, 1995
CHARACTERISTICS: Carnivore, two-legged, about 10 m long

Allosaurus A-LO-SAW-RUS
CLASSIFICATION: Theropoda
WHERE AND WHEN: North America; Late Jurassic
CLOSEST RELATIVES: *Afrovenator, Megalosaurus*
NAMED BY: Othniel Marsh, 1877
CHARACTERISTICS: Carnivore, two-legged, about 12 m long

CLASSIFICATION: Sauropoda
WHERE AND WHEN: Midwestern North America; Late Jurassic
CLOSEST RELATIVES: *Barosaurus, Brachiosaurus, Cetiosaurus, Diplodocus, Saltasaurus*
NAMED BY: Othniel Marsh, 1877
CHARACTERISTICS: Herbivore, four-legged, about 21 m long

Apatosaurus

Avimimus AH-VEE-MIME-MUS
CLASSIFICATION: Theropoda
WHERE AND WHEN: Mongolia, Central Asia; Late Cretaceous
CLOSEST RELATIVES: ?*Struthiomimus*
NAMED BY: Sergey Kurzanov, 1981
CHARACTERISTICS: Carnivore, two-legged, about 1.5 m long

Barosaurus BA-RO-SAW-RUS
CLASSIFICATION: Sauropoda
WHERE AND WHEN: Midwestern North America and Tanzania, East Africa; Late Jurassic
CLOSEST RELATIVES: *Apatosaurus, Brachiosaurus, Cetiosaurus, Diplodocus, Saltasaurus*
NAMED BY: Othniel Marsh, 1890
CHARACTERISTICS: Herbivore, four-legged, about 25 m long

Brachiosaurus BRACK-EE-O-SAW-RUS
CLASSIFICATION: Sauropoda
WHERE AND WHEN: Midwestern North America and Tanzania, East Africa; Late Jurassic
CLOSEST RELATIVES: *Apatosaurus,*

Barosaurus, Cetiosaurus,
Diplodocus, Saltasaurus
NAMED BY: Elmer Riggs, 1903
CHARCTERISTICS: Herbivore, four-legged, about 22 m long

Ceratosaurus SER-A-TOE-SAW-RUS
CLASSIFICATION: Theropoda
WHERE AND WHEN: Midwestern North America; Late Jurassic
CLOSEST RELATIVES: *Coelophysis, Dilophosaurus*
NAMED BY: Othniel Marsh, 1884
CHARCTERISTICS: Carnivore, two-legged, about 6 m long

Cetiosaurus SEE-TEE-O-SAW-RUS
CLASSIFICATION: Sauropoda
WHERE AND WHEN: Europe; Middle Jurassic
CLOSEST RELATIVES: *Apatosaurus, Barosaurus, Brachiosaurus, Diplodocus, Saltasaurus*
NAMED BY: Richard Owen, 1842
CHARACTERISTICS: Herbivore, four-legged, 14-18 m long

Coelophysis SEE-LOW-FY-SIS
CLASSIFICATION: Theropoda
WHERE AND WHEN: New Mexico, USA; Late Triassic
CLOSEST RELATIVES: *Ceratosaurus, Dilophosaurus*
NAMED BY: Edward Cope, 1889
CHARACTERISTICS: Carnivore, two-legged, about 3 m long

Compsognathus COMP-SOG-NATH-US
CLASSIFICATION: Theropoda
WHERE AND WHEN: Germany; Late Jurassic
CLOSEST RELATIVES: *?Deinonychus, Velociraptor*
NAMED BY: Andreas Wagner, 1859
CHARACTERISTICS: Carnivore, two-legged, 1.4 m long

Deinonychus DIE-NO-NIKE-US
CLASSIFICATION: Theropoda
WHERE AND WHEN: Montana and Wyoming, USA; Early Cretaceous
CLOSEST RELATIVES: *?Compsognathus,*

Velociraptor
NAMED BY: John Ostrom, 1969
CHARACTERISTICS: Carnivore, two-legged, about 3 m long

Dilophosaurus DIE-LOFF-O-SAW-RUS
CLASSIFICATION: Theropoda
WHERE AND WHEN: North America; Early Jurassic
CLOSEST RELATIVES: *Ceratosaurus, Coelophysis*
NAMED BY: Sam Welles, 1970
CHARACTERISTICS: Carnivore, two-legged, about 6 m long

Diplodocus DI-PLOD-O-KUS
CLASSIFICATION: Sauropoda
WHERE AND WHEN: Midwestern North America; Late Jurassic
CLOSEST RELATIVES: *Apatosaurus, Barosaurus, Brachiosaurus, Cetiosaurus, Saltasaurus*
NAMED BY: Othniel Marsh, 1878
CHARACTERISTICS: Herbivore, four-legged, about 27 m long

Eoraptor EE-O-RAP-TOR
CLASSIFICATION: Theropoda
WHERE AND WHEN: Argentina; Late Triassic
CLOSEST RELATIVE: *Herrerasaurus*
NAMED BY: Paul Sereno, 1993
CHARACTERISTICS: Carnivore, two-legged, about 1 m long

Euoplocephalus

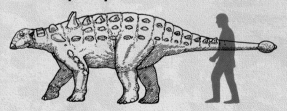

Euoplocephalus YOU-OPP-LOW-SEFF-A-LUS
CLASSIFICATION: Ankylosauria
WHERE AND WHEN: Midwestern North America; Late Cretaceous
CLOSEST RELATIVE: *Scelidosaurus*
NAMED BY: Lawrence Lambe, 1910
CHARACTERISTCS: Herbivore, four-legged, about 6 m long

Heterodontosaurus HET-ER-O-DON-TOE-SAW-RUS
CLASSIFICATION: Ornithopod
WHERE AND WHEN: South Africa; Early Jurassic
CLOSEST RELATIVES: *Hypsilophodon, Iguanodon, Leaellynasaura*
NAMED BY: A W Crompton and Alan Charig, 1962
CHARACTERISTICS: Herbivore, two-legged, 1.2 m long

Heterodontosaurus

Hypsilophodon HIP-SEE-LOFF-OH-DON
CLASSIFICATION: Ornithopod
WHERE AND WHEN: England; Early Cretaceous
CLOSEST RELATIVES: *Iguanodon, Leaellynasaura, Muttaburrasaurus, Tenontosaurus*
NAMED BY: Thomas Huxley, 1870
CHARACTERISTICS: Herbivore, two-legged, about 2 m long

Iguanodon IG-WA-NO-DON
CLASSIFICATION: Ornithopod
WHERE AND WHEN: England; Early Cretaceous
CLOSEST RELATIVES: *Heterodontosaurus, Hypsilophodon, Leaellynasaura, Muttaburrasaurus*
NAMED BY: Gideon Mantell, 1825
CHARACTERISTICS: Herbivore, two-legged, about 10 m long

Leaellynasaura LEE-ELL-IN-A-SAW-RA
CLASSIFICATION: Ornithopod
WHERE AND WHEN: Australia; Early Cretaceous
CLOSEST RELATIVES: *Heterodontosaurus, Hypsilophodon, Iguanodon, Muttaburrasaurus*
NAMED BY: Tom and Pat Rich, 1989
CHARACTERISTICS: Herbivore, two-legged, about 2 m long

Lexovisaurus LEX-O-VEE-SAW-RUS
CLASSIFICATION: Stegosaur
WHERE AND WHEN: Europe; Middle Jurassic
CLOSEST RELATIVES: *Scelidosaurus, Stegosaurus*
NAMED BY: Robert Hoffstetter, 1957
CHARACTERISTICS: Herbivore, four-legged, about 5 m long

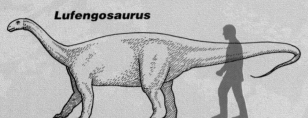
Lufengosaurus

Lufengosaurus LOO-FENG-GO-SAW-RUS
CLASSIFICATION: Prosauropod
WHERE AND WHEN: China; Early Jurassic
CLOSEST RELATIVES: *Massospondylus, Plateosaurus*
NAMED BY: C C Young, 1941
CHARACTERISTICS: Herbivore, two- or four-legged, about 6 m long

Maiasaura MY-A-SAW-RA
CLASSIFICATION: Ornithopod
WHERE AND WHEN: Midwestern North America; Late Cretaceous
CLOSEST RELATIVES: *Parasaurolophus, Saurolophus*
NAMED BY: Jack Horner and Robert Makela, 1979
CHARACTERISTICS: Herbivore, two-legged, no crest, about 9 m long

Massospondylus MASS-O-SPON-DEE-LUS
CLASSIFICATION: Prosauropod
WHERE AND WHEN: South Africa; Early Jurassic
CLOSEST RELATIVES: *Lufengosaurus, Plateosaurus*
NAMED BY: Richard Owen, 1854
CHARACTERISTICS: Herbivore, two- or four-legged, about 4 m long

Megalosaurus MEG-A-LO-SAW-RUS
CLASSIFICATION: Theropoda

WHERE AND WHEN: Europe; Middle Jurassic
CLOSEST RELATIVES: *Afrovenator, Allosaurus*
NAMED BY: William Buckland, 1824
CHARACTERISTICS: Carnivore, two-legged, about 9 m long

Muttaburrasaurus MOO-TA-BURR-A-SAW-RUS
CLASSIFICATION: Ornithopod
WHERE AND WHEN: Australia; Early Cretaceous
CLOSEST RELATIVES: *Hypsilophodon, Iguanodon, Leaellynasaura, Tenontosaurus*
NAMED BY: A Bartholomai and Ralph Molnar, 1981
CHARACTERISTICS: Herbivore, two-legged, about 7 m long

Oviraptor O-VEE-RAP-TOR
CLASSIFICATION: Theropoda
WHERE AND WHEN: Mongolia, Central Asia; Late Cretaceous
CLOSEST RELATIVE: ?*Struthiomimus*
NAMED BY: Henry Osborn, 1924
CHARACTERISTICS: Carnivore, two-legged, about 2 m long

Pachycephalosaurus PACK-EE-SEFF-A-LO-SAW-RUS
CLASSIFICATION: Pachycephalosaur
WHERE AND WHEN: Midwestern North America; Late Cretaceous
CLOSEST RELATIVES: Other pachycephalosaurs, ceratopsians
NAMED BY: Barnum Brown and E M Schlaikjer, 1943
CHARACTERISTICS: Herbivore, two-legged, about 8 m long

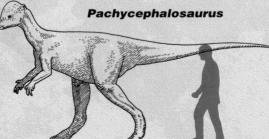
Pachycephalosaurus

Parasaurolophus PARA-SAW-O-LOAF-US
CLASSIFICATION: Ornithopod

WHERE AND WHEN: Midwestern North America; Late Cretaceous
CLOSEST RELATIVES: *Maiasaura, Saurolophus*
NAMED BY: W Parks, 1923
CHARACTERISTICS: Herbivore, two-legged, about 10 m long

Plateosaurus PLAT-EE-O-SAW-RUS
CLASSIFICATION: Prosauropod
WHERE AND WHEN: Europe; Late Triassic
CLOSEST RELATIVES: *Lufengosaurus, Massospondylus*
NAMED BY: Hermann von Meyer, 1837
CHARACTERISTICS: Herbivore, two- or four-legged, 6-8 m long

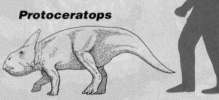
Protoceratops

Protoceratops PRO-TOE-SERR-A-TOPS
CLASSIFICATION: Ceratopsian
WHERE AND WHEN: Mongolia, Central Asia; Late Cretaceous
CLOSEST RELATIVES: *Triceratops*
NAMED BY: William Gregory and Walter Granger, 1923
CHARACTERISTICS: Herbivore, four-legged, 1.8 m long

Saltasaurus SALL-TA-SAW-RUS
CLASSIFICATION: Sauropoda
WHERE AND WHEN: Argentina; Late Cretaceous
CLOSEST RELATIVES: *Apatosaurus, Barosaurus, Brachiosaurus, Cetiosaurus, Diplodocus*
NAMED BY: José Bonaparte and Jaime Powell, 1980
CHARACTERISTICS: Herbivore, four-legged, about 12 m long

Saurolophus SAW-RO-LOAF-US
CLASSIFICATION: Ornithopod
WHERE AND WHEN: Midwestern North America and Mongolia; Late Cretaceous

CLOSEST RELATIVES: *Maiasaura,*
Parasaurolophus
NAMED BY: Barnum Brown, 1912
CHARACTERISTICS: Herbivore, two-
legged, 9-12 m long

Scelidosaurus SKEL-IDE-O-SAW-RUS

CLASSIFICATION: ?Stego-Ankylosaur
WHERE AND WHEN: England; Early
Jurassic
CLOSEST RELATIVES: *Lexovisaurus,*
Stegosaurus
NAMED BY: Richard Owen, 1859
CHARACTERISTICS: Herbivore, four-
legged, about 4 m long

Stegosaurus STEG-O-SAW-RUS

CLASSIFICATION: Stegosaur
WHERE AND WHEN: Midwestern
North America; Late Jurassic
CLOSEST RELATIVES: *Lexovisaurus,*
Scelidosaurus
NAMED BY: Othniel Marsh, 1877
CHARACTERISTICS: Herbivore, four-
legged, about 7 m long

Stegosaurus

Struthiomimus STROOTH-EE-O-MIME-US

CLASSIFICATION:: Theropoda
WHERE AND WHEN: Midwestern
North America; Late Cretaceous
CLOSEST RELATIVES: ?*Avimimus*
NAMED BY: Henry Osborn, 1917
CHARACTERISTICS: Carnivore, two-
legged, 3-4 m long

Tarbosaurus TAR-BO-SAW-RUS

CLASSIFICATION: Theropoda
WHERE AND WHEN: Mongolia,
Central Asia; Late Cretaceous
CLOSEST RELATIVE: *Tyrannosaurus*
NAMED BY: Evgeny Maleev, 1955

CHARACTERISTICS: Carnivore, two-
legged, 10-14 m long

Tenontosaurus TEN-ON-TOE-SAW-RUS

CLASSIFICATION: Ornithopod
WHERE AND WHEN: Midwestern
North America; Early Cretaceous
CLOSEST RELATIVES: *Hypsilophodon,*
Iguanodon, Leaellynasaura
NAMED BY: Barnum Brown, 1903
CHARACTERISTICS: Herbivore, two-
legged, about 6.5 m long

Triceratops TRY-SERR-A-TOPS

CLASSIFICATION: Ceratopsian
WHERE AND WHEN: Midwestern
North America; Late Cretaceous
CLOSEST RELATIVES: *Protoceratops*
NAMED BY: Othniel Marsh, 1889
CHARACTERISTICS: Herbivore, four-
legged, three horns on face, about
9 m long

Troodon TROE-O-DON

CLASSIFICATION: Theropoda
WHERE AND WHEN: Mongolia,
Central Asia; Late Cretaceous
CLOSEST RELATIVES: ?*Deinonychus*
NAMED BY: Joseph Leidy, 1856
CHARACTERISTICS: Carnivore,
two-legged, 2.4 m long

Tyrannosaurus TIE-RAN-O-SAW-RUS

CLASSIFICATION: Theropoda
WHERE AND WHEN: Midwestern
North America; Late Cretaceous
CLOSEST RELATIVES: *Tarbosaurus*
NAMED BY: Henry Osborn, 1905
CHARACTERISTICS: Carnivore, two-
legged, 14 m long

Velociraptor VEL-LOSS-SEE-RAP-TOR

CLASSIFICATION: Theropoda
WHERE AND WHEN: Mongolia,
Central Asia; Late Cretaceous
CLOSEST RELATIVES: ?*Compsognathus,*
Deinonychus
NAMED BY: Henry Osborn, 1924
CHARACTERISTICS: Carnivore, two-
legged, 2 m long

Websites

There are thousands of sites on the
Worldwide Web that deal with
dinosaurs. Here are 12 of the best:

**American Museum of Natural
History, New York**
http://www.amnh.org/
**Carnegie Museum of Natural
History, Pittsburg**
http://www.clpgh.org/cmnh/
Dinobase: *a complete listing of
dinosaurs and basic data*
http://palaeo.gly.bris.ac.uk/dinobase/
dinopage.html
Dinosaur Society
http://www.dinosociety.org/
**Field Museum of Natural
History, Chicago**
http://www.uic.edu/orgs/paleo/home
page.html
**Museum of Paleontology,
Berkeley, California**
http://www.ucmp.berkeley.edu/
**Natural History Museum,
London**
http://www.nhm.ac.uk/
**New Mexico Museum of
Natural History, Albuquerque**
http://www.nmmnh-abq.mus.nm.us/
nmmnh/nmmnh.html
Paleonet, *a server for all
palaeontologists*
http://www.ucmp.berkeley.edu/paleo
net/ *(for users in North America)*
http://www.nhm.ac.uk/paleonet/ *(for
users elsewhere)*
**Royal Tyrrell Museum of
Paleontology, Drumheller,
Canada**
http://tyrrell.magtech.ab.ca/
**Smithsonian Institution,
Washington, D.C.**
http://www.pvisuals.com/dinosaur_
museum/dinosaur_museum.html
**Society of Vertebrate
Paleontology**
http://eteweb.lscf.ucsb.edu/svp/

Glossary

ammonite

ammonite An extinct shellfish with a coiled shell that lived during the Mesozoic era.

amphibian An animal that lives in water and on land, including modern frogs and salamanders and their ancestors. Amphibians were the first land vertebrates.

animatronic model A robot or moving model.

ankylosaur An armoured dinosaur with bony plates on its back (some also had a knobbly tail club), from Mid Jurassic to Late Cretaceous.

borehole A small hole drilled down through the Earth's crust to see what the rocks look like.

carnivore A flesh-eating animal.

cast An impression of a bone or skeleton, either in the rock or made from plaster in the laboratory.

ceratopsian A 'horned-faced' ornithischian dinosaur, from a group known only in the Cretaceous period.

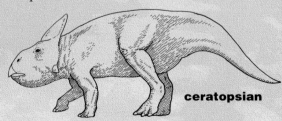

ceratopsian

cold-blooded Lacking internal control of body temperature. Modern fishes and reptiles are cold-blooded.

continental drift The slow movement of continents over the surface of the Earth.

coprolite Fossil dung.

core The centre of the Earth, made from heavy metals.

Cretaceous The time from 150 to 65 million years ago, at the end of the Mesozoic era.

crust The outer rocky layer of the Earth.

duckbill A hadrosaur, a plant-eating ornithopod from the Late Cretaceous period.

duckbill

evolution The change in plants and animals over time.

excavation Digging up a skeleton or other remains from the past.

extinction Dying out, when a species of plant or animal disappears for ever.

field Where the rocks and fossils are situated. 'Fieldwork' means going out to study the rocks.

fossil The remains of an animal or plant that lived long ago.

gastrolith A stone swallowed by a dinosaur (or a bird) to help it grind up the food in its stomach.

geology The study of rocks.

grid A pattern of equal-sized squares set up over a fossil site to help with mapping.

hadrosaur A duck-billed dinosaur, from a group of ornithopods known only from the Late Cretaceous.

herbivore A plant-eating animal.

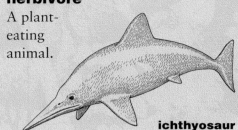

ichthyosaur

ichthyosaur A dolphin-shaped, flesh-eating reptile that lived in the Mesozoic seas. Ichthyosaurs hunted ammonites, belemnites and fishes.

impact When something hits something else hard, such as a meteorite hitting the Earth.

Jurassic The time from 205 to 150 million years ago, in the middle of the Mesozoic era.

KT boundary The Cretaceous-Tertiary boundary, the exact timeline marking the end of the dinosaurs.

magma Molten rock in the mantle of the Earth. It is called lava when it pours out of a volcano.

mammal A hairy animal that feeds its young on milk. This group of warm-blooded vertebrates includes humans, cats, bats and whales. Mammals appeared during the Late Triassic period, at about the same time as the dinosaurs.

mantle The inner part of the Earth, made from molten rock, or magma.

Mesozoic era The 'age of the dinosaurs', the time from 250 to 65 million years ago, made up of the Triassic, Jurassic and Cretaceous periods.

meteorite A rock that hurtles through space and hits the Earth.

meteorite

missing link A fossil form that is intermediate (lies between) two other groups. Missing links provide evidence for how one group, such as reptiles, evolves into another, such as birds.

mosasaur A large flesh-eating lizard that lived in the late Cretaceous seas and hunted fishes and ammonites.

ornithischian Dinosaurs with a 'bird-like' arrangement of hip bones, with the pubis sloping backwards instead of forwards.

ornithopod A two-legged, plant-eating ornithischian dinosaur, with no particular armour.

overburden The rock that lies over the top of a fossil site.

pachycephalosaur A two-legged, plant-eating ornithischian dinosaur that had a thickened skull roof. Pachycephalosaurs are known only from the Cretaceous period.

palaeontologist A person who collects and studies fossils.

palaeontology The study of fossils.

Pangaea 'All-Earth', the great supercontinent that existed in the Permian and early Mesozoic eras, when all the continents were joined together as one landmass.

pedestal A platform of rock beneath a fossil. Trenches are hacked round dinosaur bones so that they may be plastered and removed.

Permian The time from 286 to 250 million years ago, before the age of the dinosaurs.

plate tectonics The processes in the Earth's mantle and crust that cause the movement of continents.

plesiosaur

plesiosaur A long-necked, flesh-eating reptile that lived in Jurassic and Cretaceous seas. Plesiosaurs fed on fishes, and larger ones fed on other marine reptiles.

prosauropod A large, plant-eating dinosaur with a long neck that walked on two legs or on all fours. Prosauropods lived in the Late Triassic and Early Jurassic.

prospecting Searching for fossils by walking backwards and forwards over likely rocks.

pterosaur A flying reptile with wings made from skin stretched along the arm and long fourth finger.

pterosaur

pubis The bone at the front of the hip region, beneath the backbone.

radioactivity The chemical activity of certain materials that break down over time and give off energy.

raptor A small, active, flesh-eating theropod with tearing claws. Raptors lived in the Cretaceous period.

reptile The cold-blooded vertebrates that have scales and lay their eggs on dry land.

saurischian Dinosaurs with a 'lizard-hip', with the pubis pointing forwards, and a hand with a broad clawed thumb.

sauropod A large, plant-eating dinosaur that walked on four legs, and had a long neck and long tail. Sauropods were descended from the prosauropods.

sauropodomorph A plant-eating saurischian dinosaur, usually divided into prosauropods and sauropods.

stegosaur

stegosaur A 'plated reptile' with bony plates and spines along the mid-line of its back and tail.

theropod A two-legged, flesh-eating saurischian dinosaur.

Triassic The time from 250 to 205 million years ago, at the beginning of the Mesozoic era.

tsunami A massive tidal wave set off by an impact, an earthquake or the eruption of a volcano.

turbinates Thin bones inside the nose of birds and animals. They are covered with skin and help to save heat being lost through the nose.

type specimen The first specimen of a species to be given a name.

tyrannosaur A large, flesh-eating theropod of a group known only in the late Cretaceous period.

tyrannosaur tooth

vertebrate An animal with a backbone.

warm-blooded Having internal control of body temperature.

Index

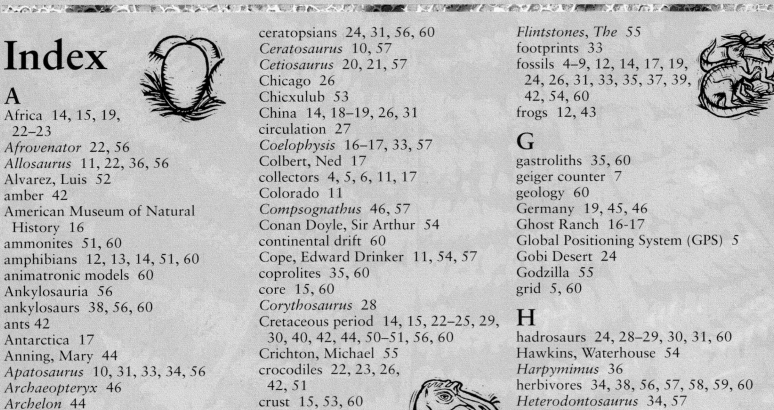

Acknowledgements

The publishers would like to thank the following
illustrators for their contributions to this book:

Jim Channel (Bernard Thornton Artists) 19*br*, 23*c*, 24*cl*, 28*bl*, 29*br*,
33*b*, 36*br*, 40*cl*; 44*tr*, 45; James Field (Simon Girling & Associates)
10–13, 16–17, 18, 24–25, 32, 35*bl*, 36–37, 40–43, 46*l*, 56–61;
Bernard Gudynas 52–53; Tim Hayward (Bernard Thornton Artists)
28–29*t*, 30, 31*tr*, 38–39, 47*t*, 50*b*, 50–51*t*; Christian Hook 4–9,
25*tr*, *cr*, *br*, 44*bl*; Mark Iley 18*bl*, 23*br*, 25*tl*, 31*c*, 34*tr*, 35*tl*,
36*tr*, 38*tl*, *bc*, 39*c*, *cr*, 41*br*, 47*b*; Martin Knowelden
(Virgil Pomfret Agency) 18–19, 34–35, 48–49;
Denis Ovenden 26–27; Tim Slade 14–15,26*bl*,
29*cl*, 33*cl*, 35*tr*, 40*bl*, 45*br*, 48*bl*, 51*tr*, 56*tl*.

Decorative border by Chris Forsey
Black-and-white *Maiasaura* icons by Rosamund Fowler
(Artist Partners Ltd)

The publishers would also like to thank the following for
supplying photographs for this book:

American Museum of Natural History, neg. no. 312 408, courtesy Dept. of
Library Services 11*br*; American Museum of Natural History / Mongolian
Academy / Dr Michael Novacek 2*bl*; Professor Michael Benton 41*c*;
Colorific / Matrix / Louis Psihoyos 12*tr*, 55*tc*; Corbis / David Muench 4*bl*;
Corbis / U.P.I. 17*br*; Corbis 26*br*; Corbis / Tom Bean 33*tr*; Corbis /
Jonathan Blair 51*br*; Corbis / Gail Mooney 55*cr*; D.C. Comics / Hanna
Barbera Production Company 55*tr*; Mary Evans Picture Library 54*tl*, 54*tr*;
Ronald Grant Archive 54*br*, 54–55*c*, 55*bl*; Professor Kielan Jaworowska /
Polish Academy of Sciences / Instiutute of Paleobiology, Warsaw 37*t*; Natural
History Museum, London 17*tr*, 24*tr*, 31*br*, 35*br*, 39*tl*, 42*bl*;
Robert Opie 55*br*; Peabody Museum of Natural History, Yale University
11*cr*; Frank Spooner Pictures / Xinhua-Chine 19*tr*, Frank Spooner Pictures
23*tr*; Tony Stone Images 54*cr*